Warrior Dreams
A Journal to Inspire Your Fiercely Alive Whole Self

Other titles by Laura Di Franco Probert

Memoir
Living, Healing and Taekwondo

Poetry
Warrior Love, A Journal to Inspire Your Fiercely Alive Whole Self
Warrior Joy, A Journal to Inspire Your Fiercely Alive Whole Self
Warrior Soul, A Journal to Inspire Your Fiercely Alive Whole Self

Contributor for
What's In Your Web, Stories of Fascial Freedom
Superwoman Myths, Break the Rules of Silence and Speak Up Your Truth
365 Ways to Connect With Your Soul

Copyright ©2017 by Laura Probert. All rights reserved. No portions of this book, except for brief reviews, may be reproduced, stored in a retrieval system, or transmitted in any form or by any means-electronic, mechanical, photocopying, recording or otherwise-without the written permission of the publisher. For information contact CreateSpace.

Published July 7, 2017 by CreateSpace

Cover artwork: Moon Child, by Laura Di Franco Probert

ISBN-13: 978-1548389093
ISBN- 10: 1548389099

Warrior Dreams

A Journal to Inspire Your Fiercely Alive Whole Self

by Laura Di Franco Probert

Warrior Dreams, a Journal to Inspire Your Fiercely Alive Whole Self is the fourth journal in a series born when I stood up in front of two hundred and twenty people, read aloud from my journal, and became a poet. This fourth journal is a collection of the poems and journaling that moved through me when I began connecting with my authentic self and deepest desires; when I became unapologetic about my dreams and made big changes in my life to honor them.

WARRIOR LOVE: An indomitable, generous and kind spirit; a sure knowing that on-purpose, positive and persistent awareness is the real fight worth fighting.

Dear Warrior Soul,

My wish is that you'll feel these poems…and then write a little bit in response to the questions on the blank pages that follow. Connect with the voice of your soul, your deepest desires, and your warrior dreams.

With Love,
Laura

for Chris

Table of Contents

I Swore I'd Never Feel

The Way You've Only Dreamed

Time to Change Your Mind

Let Joy In

Let Courage Find Me Again

Snow Falls

A Woman Falling

My New Clothes

I Promise Her The Sun

Inhale the Moon

Peace Angel

Ride the Night

So Much

When the Sky Talks

Burning Inside

Imagine a Heart

Be the Poem

What You Crave

Drunk

The Vibration of Love

I Rise and Fall

The First Firefly

I Swore I'd Never Feel

It might make you
jump for joy
send shivers of delight
up your spine.

Or disgust you
repulse you
send waves of nausea
to your throat.

No matter if it
wraps you in rapture
or
makes you wanna scream.

Even if it
tingles your soul
or
shrink wraps your heart…

Feel it
all of it
to the last drop
of feel.

Taste it
slowly
until it finally
melts away.

Touch it
everywhere
every crevice
every curve.

Hear it
carefully
listen to all
it has to say.

See it
from its essence
observe detached
and calm.

Wonder openly
stay curious
quiet
and kind.

It may take everything
you got
push every button
made.

It could send you flying
or crashing
but either way
try surfing the waves.

If you're blissed out
or livid
raged-filled
or timid.

It's all there for you
all there as food
to take you higher
make you stronger.

Even the stuff
you swore
you'd never feel
is patiently waiting for you to see.

It's all possibility
and what matters
is whether you decide
to be you and stay awake.

What are you resisting?

The Way You've Dreamed

Do the big, hard thing.
Feel how your lungs expand
with a breath so sweet
and free
you remember who you are again.

Say the thing you're afraid to say.
Feel how your body melts
with a release so warm
and deep
you believe the truth of your soul.

Dream the thing too big to dream.
Feel how your spirit catches fire
with a flame so bright
and hot
it fuels your plan to heal the world.

Choose to make joy your purpose.
Feel how your life flows
with an ease so smooth
and graceful
it reminds you of your magic.

Give yourself permission to be yourself.
Feel how your body, mind and soul align
with a power so wild
and raw
the world sits up to notice.

Do the thing
Speak your mind
Choose joy
Be yourself
Watch your journey unfold
the way you've dreamed it could be.

If I weren't afraid, I would_____.

Time to Change Your Mind

Standing on the lofty magic
of surrender
my steps are more sure
than ever
before.

Unchained from worry
and doubt
my breath carries me further
than I've ever
been.

With presence by my side
holding her hand
my heart is more open
than when
I was a child.

I'm riding a wave of joy
today
that's the most certain thing
I've known
in a while.

I stand rubbing my wrists
where the marks
remind me
of how I never want to live
again.

The rest of my life holds promise
waves of bliss
an unwavering faith
I wade, smiling
waiting.

I'm yours right now
in my truth
my soul rich with healed wounds
my fucks-to-give factor
low.

It's time to ride
time to laugh
time to sing and dance
time to order everything
on the menu.

Waking up on the wings of now
naked, wild and free
I see
the miracle
and it's time to claim it for my own.

This life's for living
fiercely alive
in uninhibited vibrations of love
luminescent beams of light
dialed up on rapture.

Your fear is boring
Your problems are small
Your resentment is suffocating
Your negativity is toxic
and your mind knows how to change it all.

Time to change your mind.

What's something you need to change your mind about?

Let Joy In

Scoop up love
hold as much as you can
pour it into the spots
corroded by shame
leave blame
in the wake
you make
as you create your wave
essence the effervescence
glowing under the moon
your soul the tide
ebb and flow
release and know
you're meant for more
and love
is the way.

Scoop again
and sip
from your hands
drink in what you need
to quench
your thirst
your search ends
here at this turn
let your knees

meet the earth
as you offer
what no longer serves
to the wind
feel the pain
lift
and joy seep in.

I feel the most joy when_____.

Let Courage Find Me Again

I see you standing there
bare.
The Winter trees aren't enough
to keep you hidden
as you prefer.

I see you moving forward
anyway.
Fear isn't big enough
to keep you helpless
like before.

I hear your voice now;
strong.
Wind carries your shame away,
keeps you powerful
like you were meant to be.

I feel your soul here,
indomitable.
Presence fuels your fire
to keep you purposeful
like your heart enjoys.

I close my eyes
against the warm morning breeze,
fingers outstretched to receive,
face toward the moon to believe
and pray…

Please let me know
my way.
Let me be clear most days
let the moon, stars and wind
speak their love through me.

Let me be useful
today.
Allow me to discipline my mind
let kindness rule
and courage find me again.

Help me feel
I'm enough
when I can't see,
to keep me the Goddess
I was born to be.

I connect most with my intuition when_____.

Snow Falls

Snow falls
children sleep and dream
as I sit watching
wondering how much
wondering if
wondering how.

The blanket settles
birds hide and burrow
as I sit watching
getting still
getting nervous
getting brave.

The day softens
plans are derailed
as I sit watching
breathing
practicing
noticing.

Words flow
my mind clears
as I sit watching
smiling
knowing
being.

When I get still I _____.

A Woman Falling

A woman
falling into herself
finally owning her worth
body, mind and soul…
this woman is powerful.

She breathes love
sweats courage
eats passion
and drinks bliss.

A woman
nourished by her own light
stoked by her sensuality
filled up by her own inspiration…
this woman's unstoppable

She sees joy
hears opportunity
feels everything
and lives on those edges.

A woman
coming fiercely alive
by the sheer ache of her soul
decides to listen…
this woman's a priestess.

She casts spells
creates magic
knows things
and follows her own rules.

A woman
jumping off the ledge
free falling into uncertainty
quickly learns to fly…
this woman is brave.

She recognizes doubt
feels fear
calls out shame
and chooses love.

A woman
becoming a warrior
no longer afraid to speak
her wild, real voice…
this woman is here.

She wants rapture
demands respect
takes no shit
and she's ready to change the world.

When I fall into myself I _____.

My New Clothes

I hardly recognize myself.
The good girl who followed the rules
cared what others thought
to the point of her own demise…
she's dead.

I watched as she died.
An excruciating feeling of unworthiness
writhed, screamed and resisted
until the end
until something bigger happened.

I was curious in new skin.
A demon-like force of LOVE emerged,
took over the tentative, hesitant, fear-ridden girl,
made sure she stood tall,
walked her walk.

I'm wearing new clothes
feeling a tighter fit
they make me feel sexy
and sure
Priestess-like.

I'm wearing my hair down.
I understand the power of confidence
from essence unleashed,
fueled by joy, love, rapture
and color.

I'm now becoming me
unpredictable, awake
I'm not the best friend, lover
or co-worker
if you're still afraid.

I'm now a beaming, blinding light
every irresponsible decision un-judged
every act of love
a force to be reckoned with,
honored.

And…if you're still afraid
you might get burned being with me.
If you're curious,
you might find yourself in me
and everything will start to change.

Where or with who are you not being your true self?

I Promise Her The Sun

A steady rain comes
pouring over my decision
dampening the air
making things less clear

Gentle splattering
makes a sound so real
I think everything is wet
and grey is the color of the sky

Even the dogs sit safe
behind the threshold
unwilling to venture out
an instinct to stay

I sit behind the same line
watching, taking notes
wondering what's real, what's wet
imagining how to stay dry

I feel the why behind caution
I see the danger in going out
I know I could be deceived
I understand what wet means

But there's birth in the rain
necessary for growth
a must for survival
a dark creating light

I'm questioning the very thing
that makes miracles
the only thing
that creates life

I let the rain come
feel the cold, damp
open up my pores
let it soak my soul

Because I know about the seed
sitting patiently beneath
consolidated joy
counting on me

I let the rain come
feel every drop
surrender myself again
and promise her the sun.

When has the dark allowed you to see more light?

Inhale the Moon

Inhale the morning
exhale the shift
baking in your bones
time travels quickly
in bursts and torturous moments
either way you'll feel
or not
quake with unknown sensation
or lie dead with numbness
either way
you can't mess it up.

Inhale the moon
exhale the transformation
blazing in your blood
dreams fade un-noticeably
in unconscious mistakes
either way you'll feel
or not
tighten it all down
or scream bloody, wild Hell
either way
you can't mess it up.

When do you choose staying numb? Why?

Peace Angel

I find you in my dreams
in my bed
on my mind

I find my heart
blown apart
by your kindness

Your smile's an anchor
that floats to me
out at sea

I found my soul
stretched out
over your laughter

I pick up pieces
of my life
you've let me drop
without a fight

We look at them
through your lens
the view changes
in full color

I get why you came
nothing could be the same
if I wanted
a forever change

I had to learn the truth
feel it deeply for myself
know the difference
between Heaven and Hell

Taking your hand
walking through fire
my wings unfold

You've shown me
I can survive
If I rise and fly

You've helped me know
the powerful force
that's me

My angel for sure
pure peace arrives
and everything's alright

What happens when your perspective changes?

Ride the Night

Ride the night
in shadowy dreams
sparkling bright
with hope

Coast along
in visions with all
the dazzling souls
who believe

Sail away
in coconut-coated breezes
teasing you out
of your skin

and then

Light the sky
with fiery promises
spilling diamonds
onto yourself

Dance into your future
outstretched and expectant
patiently anxious
with knowing

Speak it all up
with fierce love and gratitude
radiating yeses
to your desires

Exude your heat
with eyes and heart
tempting essence
to steal the show

Move in the world
in moments and bites
mindful delights
only meant for joy

Live now or never
in raw, true you
taste the salt of wonder
along the rim of doubt

and then

Breathe the uncertainty
with chocolate-covered presence
sucking slowly
revealing its crunchy core

Eat some more
with a curious tongue and mind
find the time
to savor your pain

Hold your secrets
with ease and grace
lifting them to the wind
for release

Ride the night
in dark, sweet dreams
lingering shivers through your spine
it's time to be.

It's time to be fiercely alive.

What makes you feel alive?

So Much

Have you ever
loved something so much
you lose track of time
your soul
unwinding
moments,
JOY
bubbling up
to dance
beneath your skin
presence staying
so clear
and fierce
you forget
for a second
where you are
your duties
crumbling
under the weightlessness
of bliss
life
becoming
the most magical
badass place
to play
you've ever known?
Have you ever?

What do you love to do so much you lose track of time?

When the Sky Talks

When the Sky talks
in creeping moonlit clouds
splatter-painted stars
and midnight hues
I must be
the audience she sees
waiting for something grand
hoping for no finale
but an endless show.

I sit myself down
supported for hours
of upward gaze
inhales deeper
expectations more attached.

The sky would never
let me down.

She knows I only come
when my soul's at stake
when I need to believe
in something more
sure.

Looking up
is how I feel inside
light in the dark
quiet chaos
the place I know
things fly.

When the sky talks
and she always does
she reminds me what matters
grounds me in magic
tells me
one more time
I'm more than all this
and sends me goodnight
with a kiss sweeter than any lover.

A touch so pure
my velvet-coated dreams
sing to me
and my silvery essence
can finally rest
in her deep shadows.

The sky talks
and when I listen
more good things happen
in the time it takes

one passing cloud
to move out of view
than in a decade of thinking.

And I begin to think
I should come talk more often.

When I connect with nature I_____.

Burning Inside

When you're burning inside
hiding
some part of your life
wanting to show the world
as usual
smothering your soul
instead

Feel the dread
in your gut
don't put up
with that stuff
you're meant to live
fully alive

Notice the ways
you play the game
like everyone says
and go against the very thing
that lights you up
and let's you shine

See how you're killing
yourself slowly
only going where
you're led
by someone else's rules
not using your own tools

Be brave
don't settle
say the thing that needs to be said
make courage your bed
live the way you're meant to…

Joyful, wild and free.

How have you been hiding?

Imagine a Heart

Imagine a heart
ready for anything
not worried about the future
or things of the past
a wild, free heart
unencumbered by fear
an open vessel for love

Imagine a heart
ready for anything
not shamed about mistakes
or judgmental of failures
an open, compassionate heart
a place for natural presence

Imagine a heart
ready for anything
not attached to an outcome
or expectations
a creative, flowing heart
unamused by drama

Imagine a heart
ready for anything
all the sorrow and all the joy
all that's pure love

a perfect, wounded heart
strengthened by vulnerability

Imagine a heart
ready for anything
awake for everything
with an intention of gratitude
a fearless, passionate heart
connected to the truth of her longing.

What would your heart say to you?

Be the Poem

You're poetry
to my soul
stroking my skin
with your smile
warm breath
on my neck.

How you stay here
no matter what
holding space
for my tears
knowing just when
and where to touch.

When your eyes say
everything I need to hear
it's clear
you are a poem
in my world
and I'll play
in the rhythm and rhyme
of you
for as long as time
syncing my beat
with yours
for a chance at a glimpse

of your essence
as she dances around my heart
breathes life into my cells
and pulls the wild girl
out for a spin.

Your poem
stands in front of me
arms crossed
legs firm
and says softly,
"When will you see, sweet thing,"
"You are the poem."
"You are the essence of love."
"It's time to live inside
of your own prose."

So lay down your pen
let the words flow
from your heart to your tongue,
allow what's done to be done
let your soul speak
the rapturous dreams
you seek.
Be the poem.

What are your dreams made of?

What You Crave

What you crave -
that's souls' desire.
Who are you
to mess with her fire?

Feed the flame
burning your core.
Life's too short,
it's okay to want more.

Connect with her
she'll help you see
everything
you're meant to be.

What you've smothered
for so long
will set you free,
it's your song.

Lean in and listen.
Her sweet melody
is begging you here.
Wake up and see.

Feel the deep roots
of your desire.
Let your heart and soul
catch fire.

Move slowly now
take your time
let the rhythm
stoke the flame.

With that light
and raging heat
taste the truth
it's time to eat.

Pick up the fruit
sink your teeth in.
Let the juices
run down your chin.

What you crave…
it's meant to be tasted.
It's how you know bliss.
Please don't waste it.

Feel the fear.
Move past the thoughts.
Step into your power.
This's your shot.

What you crave
is soul's sweet desire.
It's time to build
one huge, badass fire.

My biggest desires are_____.

Drunk

Officer, I'm drunk;
under the influence
of the moon and stars tonight
drinking oversized gulps
of their magic.

Lock me up.
I'm so far gone
I'm a danger to others;
could love too hard
at any moment.

Throw away the key
cuz I'm happy in this place
crazed and dazed by the light
a bad girl forever
doomed to fall again and again.

Where are you holding back your love?

The Vibration of Love

from the sacred moonlit night
she rose
from the soft pink sunrise
she rose
from the warm, rugged earth
she rose
from her soul's flaming essence
she rose
and ignited a revolution;
brave
worthy
out loud
purposeful
positive
generous
and aware…
she rose, lit from within
shining out
feeling everything
healing everything
living the joy
honoring the pain
touching stillness
allowing the vibration
of love
to rule.

Why not you?

I Rise and Fall

I rise
and fall
like breath
~life itself~

Time to honor
all of it
for the perfection
it is

One
without the other
doesn't
work

One
without the other
means
death

I rise
and fall
naturally
unconsciously

Time to trust
both
remember both
are necessary

I rise
and
I fall
like breath

Neither
more valuable
neither
less than

I'm alive
in both
I thrive
because of both

The only options?
jump higher
crash harder
breathe deeper

How do you react in the rise and fall moments?

The First Firefly

The first firefly
always
catches my eye

It's time
to light up
the night
when June's
sweet wet heat
covers the grass
and dusk
takes it's time
to arrive

My heart
lightens
with the extra
time to play
and my soul
wants to stay
a little longer
to walk
with the breeze

I sit still
to watch
my magical friends
call
each other
in Summer's
brightest
love dance

My eyes
fall victim
to the trance
of the first
firefly…
my chance
to believe
in the small
miracles
of life

What feels like a miracle to you?

Sending you off with big love and magical wishes for all of your warrior dreams come true. You're good enough. There's nothing standing in your way but your own beliefs. Stay awake, stay strong, and carry on with your badass self.
Laura

Thank you for reading my poems. I'd love to hear from you. You can email me at bewarriorlove@gmail.com

Come play with me online:

Website: **www.BraveHealer.com**

Brave Healer Facebook page:
www.Facebook.com/KickAssWarriorGoddess

Facebook Poetry page: **www.Facebook.com/WarriorLove**

Brave Healers are Changing the World Facebook Group:
https://www.facebook.com/groups/1469783109971221/

Twitter: **@LiveHealTKD**

Instagram: **@LauraProbert_**

Made in the USA
Columbia, SC
04 August 2018